Brazil: 62 Fascinating Facts For Kids

Shirley Lucas

This book is just one of a series of "Fascinating Facts For Kids" books. For more fascinating facts about people, history, animals and more please visit:

www.fascinatingfactsforkids.com

Contents

Where is Brazil?

1. Brazil is the largest country in the continent of South America and the fifth largest in the world, after Russia, Canada, the United States and China. It is home to a population of more than 200 million.

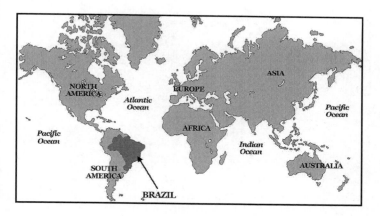

2. Brazil covers a distance of 2,689 miles (4,302 km) from east to west and almost the same distance from north to south. It has a land area of 3.3 million square miles (8.5 million square km) and shares its border with every South American country except Ecuador and Chile.

3. Brazil's coastline stretches for 4,654 miles (7,491 km) from French Guiana in the north to Uruguay in the south, along the North Atlantic and South Atlantic Oceans.

History

4.   Although South American Indians had been living for thousands of years in the area we now call Brazil, it wasn't until the 16th century that the country was born.

5.   In April 1500, a fleet of Portuguese ships commanded by Pedro Álvares Cabral landed for the first time on the shores of what is now Brazil. 30 years later the first settlers arrived and claimed the country as a colony of Portugal.

Pedro Álvares Cabral landing in Brazil

6.   The early settlers discovered a tree which produced high-quality wood and a valuable red dye. The Portuguese called this tree "Pau Brasil" and named their new country in its honor.

7. The Portuguese began to cultivate the land and they set up large plantations to grow sugar, which was a valuable product back in Europe. People were needed to work on the plantations and the 16th and 17th centuries saw millions of slaves brought across the Atlantic Ocean from Africa.

Below deck on a slave ship sailing to Brazil

8. The African slaves enabled the Portuguese to become extremely wealthy, but they endured dreadful working and living conditions. Over the years, many slaves escaped or rebelled against their masters, but it wasn't until 1888 that slavery was finally abolished in Brazil.

9. A new source of wealth came to Brazil when gold was discovered in 1695. Many mines opened and the next century saw Brazil become the world's greatest producer of gold. Thousands of prospectors flocked to Brazil to seek their fortunes, but eventually the gold started to run out and the mines began to close.

10. Brazil became an independent country in 1822 when the then Portuguese ruler, Dom Pedro, declared himself King. The monarchy lasted until 1889, when Brazil became a republic. Brazil's first elected president, Prudente de Morais, took office five years later.

Prudente de Morais

11. The end of the 19th century saw coffee growing and rubber production become huge industries in Brazil, although as with the sugar plantations, the great wealth they brought reached relatively few people.

12. The 20th century saw Brazil open its borders for people to come and work on the coffee plantations and make new lives in the ever-growing cities. Today, Brazil's population is a rich mix of people from all over the world.

Climate & Landscape

13. The vast size of Brazil means that its landscape and climate vary greatly depending on where you are in the country.

14. Half of Brazil is covered by the world's largest tropical rainforest, which is situated in the north-west of the country. The climate in this region is hot and humid, whatever the time of year. The rainforest has around 90 inches (228 cm) of rainfall every year and the average daytime temperature is 79°F (26°C).

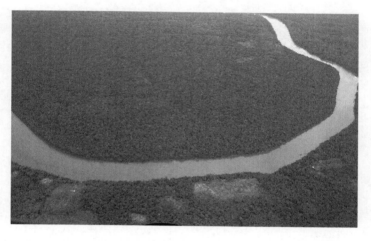

Aerial view of the Brazilian rainforest

15. The rainforest of Brazil surrounds the River Amazon, the world's second longest river after the River Nile in Africa. The Amazon is around 4,000 miles (6,400 km) long and every hour more than 200,000 gallons (640,000 l) of water pour into the Atlantic Ocean at the river's mouth.

16. The north-east of Brazil has little rainfall and has a large area of semi-desert. The region's coast is famous for its beautiful beaches and is a major tourist destination.

A beach in North-east Brazil

17. The Pantanal, which is the largest tropical wetland area in the world, is found in the west of Brazil. The Pantanal turns into a lake the size of France during the rainy season and is home to an immense variety of wildlife.

18. The south-east of Brazil is an area of rolling hills and the land is good for farming. Some of

Brazil's main cities, such as Rio de Janeiro and São Paulo, are situated on the Atlantic coast of this region.

Brazil's main cities

19. The south-west of Brazil is an area of great canyons and waterfalls. On the border with Argentina are the horseshoe-shaped Iguazu Falls, which are made up of around 275 separate waterfalls. At 1.8 miles (3 km) wide and 269 feet (82 m) high, they are wider and higher than the Niagara Falls of North America.

Iguazu Falls

Life in Brazil

20. Life in Brazil has changed a lot in recent times. In the mid-20th century, most people lived in the countryside, but nowadays around 75% of the population lives in the cities, which people moved to in search of work.

21. Many different languages are spoken in Brazil because of the diverse population, but Portuguese is the official language of the country. The only people who do not speak Portuguese are the native Indians, who have their own languages and dialects.

A native Indian mother and child

22. Although Brazil has become wealthier in recent years, there is a big gap between the rich and the poor. Many people live in the slums of the big cities and there are millions of children who are forced to live on the streets, as they have no home or parents.

23. Although Brazilian children are entitled to a free education, many have to leave school early in order to find work so they can earn money for their families.

24. Despite the difficulties and poor living conditions that many people face, Brazilians do know how to enjoy themselves. They love music, dance and especially soccer.

25. You can find Brazilians playing soccer anywhere! They play constantly on the beach or in the streets and this love of the game has helped Brazil become the most successful soccer nation in history.

Soccer on the beach

26. The Brazilian national soccer team has won the World Cup five times (as of 2019) - more than any other nation. The country has produced some of the greatest players ever to play the game, the greatest of them all being Edson Arantes do Nascimento, otherwise known as "Pelé".

Brazil soccer team, 2014

27. Brazil is famous for its music and dance. You see dancing and hear music everywhere you go, and everyone - young or old, rich or poor - seems to be joining in.

28. The music and dance of Brazil have been shaped by 500 years of European, African and native Indian influences, and the mixture of these different cultures has created a style that is purely Brazilian.

29. The most well-known exhibition of music and dance takes place every year in the city of Rio de Janeiro. The Rio Carnival is a five-day party and brings hundreds of thousands of tourists from all over the world to join the Brazilian people in their celebrations.

The Rio Carnival

The Amazon & the Rainforest

30. Tropical rainforests are found all around the world close to the equator and Brazil's Amazon Rainforest is the world's largest, covering 2.3 million square miles (six million square km). It covers nearly half of the continent of South America.

31. Rainforests are so important because all the trees and plants that grow in them convert the carbon dioxide found in the atmosphere into oxygen, which humans and other animals need to survive. More than 20% of the world's oxygen is produced by the Amazon Rainforest!

32. The trees of the rainforests help keep the world's weather in balance by drawing rainwater from the forest floor and releasing it back into the atmosphere, from where it eventually falls back again as rain. Without this constant recycling of rainwater the world would experience many more droughts than it already does.

33. Over the decades, countless trees in the rainforest have been cut down for their wood and also to clear space for farming and mining. This is a threat not only to the animals and plants that live in the forest, but also to the entire planet because of the change in climate that could happen.

34. Since the beginning of the 21st century, protected areas have been established in the rainforest. The Brazilian government has taken steps to slow down the destruction of the trees in order to protect both the wildlife and Earth's weather systems.

35. The Amazon Rainforest is home to an astonishing variety of wildlife. There are 1,300 types of birds, more than 400 types of mammals, 378 different reptiles and more than 400 amphibians. There are also 50,000 plant species and perhaps 2½ million types of insects!

36. The trees of the Amazon Rainforest are so tall and thick that much of the ground never sees any sunlight. When it rains, it takes ten minutes for the rainwater to get from the tops of the trees to the ground!

37. There are around 400 tribes of native Indians living in the rainforest, totaling about one million people. Each tribe has its own territory, language and culture, and many have never had contact with the outside world.

38. The River Amazon, which flows through the rainforest, has its source high in the Andes Mountains of Peru, just 100 miles (160 km) from the Pacific Ocean. 4,000 miles (6,400 km) further east the river spills into the Atlantic Ocean.

39. The first Europeans to discover the River Amazon were sailing 200 miles (320 km) from the South American coast when they realized their ship was actually in fresh water, even though they were so far from the shore. They set sail for the coast and found the mighty River Amazon.

40. The Amazon is deep enough and wide enough for large ships to sail from the Atlantic Ocean as far as 930 miles (1,500 km) inland to the city of Manaus. Smaller ships reach Iquitos in northern Peru, 2,300 miles (3,700 km) from the river's mouth.

Cities & Countryside

41. Brazil has some of the most populated cities in the world, with three out of every four Brazilians living in a town or city. Most of Brazil's cities are found in the south and south-east of the country.

42. The largest city in Brazil is São Paulo, and after Tokyo and Mexico City it is the third most populated city in the world. São Paulo is a modern, cosmopolitan city and a major industrial and business center.

Central São Paulo

43. Rio de Janeiro is Brazil's second largest city and one of the most beautiful in the world. Rio is wedged between the mountains and the ocean and is looked over by a gigantic statue of Jesus

Christ, which stands on top of the 2,329-feet-high (710 m) Corcovado Mountain.

Rio de Janeiro

44. Brasilia, situated 600 miles (960 km) north of Rio, was built in the 1950s and took over from Rio as the country's capital city in 1960. The architecture is modern and futuristic and the city's layout is in the shape of an airplane!

Brasilia

45. Brazil has vast areas of countryside where farming is the main source of income. Sugar used to be the most important crop, but these days coffee, oranges, bananas, cocoa and soybeans have taken over. Brazil produces more oranges and coffee beans than any other country.

46. The north-east of Brazil is the poorest part of the country with the dry, parched land making it difficult to grow crops. Farmers dig small dams to capture what little rain does fall so that they can water their fields and grow food to feed their families.

47. The huge, open grasslands of south and central Brazil are ideal for rearing cattle. South American cowboys, called "Gauchos", are used to round up the cattle, just like the cowboys of the United States did back in the 19th century. There are more than 160 million cattle in Brazil!

Food & Drink

48. The national dish of Brazil is "Feijodada", which is a stew made from meat and black beans, served with rice. The dish was first made by African slaves who took their masters' leftover food and cooked it in a big pot.

Feijodada

49. Even though Brazil is such a hot country, coffee is drunk throughout the day. Many Brazilians begin the day with a "café com leite" (coffee with hot milk). For the rest of the day a strong, black coffee known as "cafézinho" is drunk.

50. Breakfast in Brazil might consist of fruit, such as mango or pawpaw, bread and cheese, or perhaps "bolinho de chuva" which are traditional Brazilian doughnuts.

Bolinho de chuva

51. Brazilians usually have their main meal at lunchtime and eat again late in the evening at around 9.00 or 10.00 pm.

52. Brazilians have inherited a love of fish and seafood from their Portuguese ancestors. Most of the cities on Brazil's coast have fishing ports, so there is always plenty of fresh fish to eat.

53. Brazilians love to make fruit juice from the astonishing variety of fruit found all over the country. A favorite drink is "caipirinha", which is made from lime, sugar, ice and "cachaca" (sugar cane liquor).

Assorted Brazil Facts

54. The green background of the Brazilian flag represents the country's forests, and the yellow diamond, its mineral wealth. The 27 stars represent the 26 states and the one federal district. The position of the stars is how the night sky looked over Rio de Janeiro on 15 November 1889, when Brazil became a republic.

The Brazilian flag

55. Brazil has held the soccer World Cup twice, in 1950 and 2014, and in 2009 the country was chosen to host the 2016 Olympic Games.

56. Brazil's most famous ever soccer player, Pelé, first played for his country when he was just 17 years of age. During his 22-year career he scored 1,282 goals and won 53 titles, including three World Cups.

Pelé in 2008

57. Brazilians love motor sport and the country has produced many great racing drivers, including Nelson Piquet, Emerson Fittipaldi and Rubens Barrichello. The most famous driver is Ayrton Senna, who won the Formula One World Championship three times. He was killed on the racetrack at Imola, Italy, in 1994 at the age of just 34.

Ayrton Senna at the 1991 United States Grand Prix

58. The Portuguese settlers brought Christianity to Brazil and today the country is home to the largest population of Christians in the world after the United States.

59. Many Brazilians of African descent are followers of the Candomblé religion and they believe that everyone has their own personal god that guides and protects them.

60. Millions of people live in the crowded slums - known as "favelas" - of Brazil's cities. The government, with the help of the United States, has started a program of improvement by installing street lighting and sewage and waste-disposal systems.

A favela in Rio

61. The statue of Jesus Christ, called "Christ the Redeemer", which stands at the top of Corcovado Mountain and overlooks Rio de Janeiro, was built in 1931. It is 98 feet (30 m) high and the outstretched arms measure 92 feet (28 m) from fingertip to fingertip.

Christ the Redeemer

62. Brazil's tallest mountain is Pico de Neblina, whose peak is 9,823 feet (2,994 m) above sea level. Its name means "Peak of Mists" and is so called because the mountain is shrouded in cloud for most of the time. It was first climbed in 1965 by members of the Brazilian Army.

Pico de Neblina

For more in the Fascinating Facts For Kids series, please visit:

www.fascinatingfactsforkids.com

Illustration Attributions

**Pedro Álvares Cabral landing in Brazil |
Iguazu Falls**
www.goodfreephotos.com

**Below deck on a slave ship sailing to
Brazil**
Johann Moritz Rugendas [Public domain]
{{PD-1923}}

Prudente de Morais
Jornal A Semana [Public domain]
{{PD-1923}}

Aerial view of the Brazilian rainforest
Jorge.kike.medina [CC BY 3.0
(https://creativecommons.org/licenses/by/3.0)]
(changes made)

A native Indian mother and child
Cmacauley [CC BY-SA 3.0
(https://creativecommons.org/licenses/
by-sa/3.0)]
(changes made)

Soccer on the beach
bossa67 from Washington DC, United States [CC
BY 2.0
(https://creativecommons.org/licenses/by/2.0)]
(changes made)

Brazil soccer team, 2014

Danilo Borges/copa2014.gov.br Licença
Creative Commons Atribuição 3.0 Brasil [CC BY
3.0
(https://creativecommons.org/licenses/by/3.0)]

Central São Paulo

Ana Paula Hirama [CC BY-SA 2.0
(https://creativecommons.org/licenses/by-
sa/2.0)]

Rio de Janeiro

Artyominc
https://creativecommons.org/licenses/by-
sa/3.0/deed.fr
https://creativecommons.org/licenses/by-
sa/3.0/legalcode.fr

Brasilia

Fabiana Barbosa do N Silva [CC BY-SA 4.0
(https://creativecommons.org/licenses/by-
sa/4.0)]

Feijodada

Adrião [CC BY 3.0
(https://creativecommons.org/licenses/by/3.0)]

Bolinho de chuva

Domenico Citrangulo
https://creativecommons.org/licenses/by/2.0/
deed.pt
https://creativecommons.org/licenses/by/2.0/l
egalcode

Made in the USA
Middletown, DE
08 December 2019

80279938R00022